Social Media Marketing:

The Best Way To Build Your Brand! Make Passive Income, Speed Up Your Business By Gaining More Than 10k Followers, The Road To Success Begins Now.

I0504241

©By: Mohammad Alsafwani

Table of Contents

BLURB

I want to thank and congratulate you for purshing the book, *"Social Media Marketing: The Best Way To Build Your Brand! Make Passive Income, Speed Up Your Business By Gaining More Than 10k Followers, The Road To Success Begins Now.."*

This book contains proven steps and strategies when it comes to understanding of the facets of growing your business. The book tries to shed more insights on how to start your social media marketing and growup your business. Some of the mind-boggling ideas tackled here include Facebook marketing, Instagram marketing, Youtube marketing, and Twitter marketing.

If you have to live on a 9 to 5 job lifestyle, then you are in the right place to change this. The book gives you some excellent tips on how to turn the tables and leave a life free of budget constraints. Thanks again for purshing this book, I hope you enjoy it!

Introduction

Social media has taken over the world; gone are the days of door-to-door selling, big billboards or directories. If you are a business in this new social media age, your biggest task is, of course, to find customers. Earlier, businesses had to go out of their way to find and inform customers about their products. This was not just tiring and ineffective in most cases – most importantly, it cost far too much money. Businesses a decade ago used to have specific advertising money that they would keep aside, which would eventually eat up into their profits. Well, social media has completely solved that problem. In this new age, you don't have to find customers in the real world as everyone is now connected in a virtual space where almost all daily interactions take place. This virtual space has become a savior for businesses because now it's easier to find customers, you can interact directly with them, and you can also study their likes and dislikes to sell products to them. Social media is free so you don't even have to spend money to advertise.

This doesn't mean that you don't have to work hard to market your business. With the advent of social media, the field of marketing has become open to everyone; hence, it has become extremely competitive. If you want your product to stand out, you must build a brand through social media and you must stand out. Social media has immense potential to take your business to the next level, but that can only happen if you know what you're doing.

That's where this book comes in. The purpose of this book is not just to give you the basics of how social media marketing works, but to also familiarize you with different tips and tricks so that you can take your business to the next level. We are going to study different social media platforms, such as Facebook, YouTube, Instagram, etc. and look at different ways of finding marketing success on these platforms.

Chapter 1: Social Media and Business

Let's be real: you are probably already familiar with what social media is and how it works. By this point, virtually all of us have experienced social media in one way or another and we do not really need a crash course in the very basics of social media. However, social media as a marketing platform is a totally different beast altogether. If you want to use social media for marketing, you are going to need to understand how social media works for businesses, what it takes to turn them into a powerful marketing machine, and what you need to be doing to set yourself up for success.

We are going to go beyond the basics of social media and into the hot topic of how to leverage social media for marketing. You are also going to learn about how you can pick the right niche, create a strong profile, and identify the right strategy to really make the most out of your online presence. This way, no matter what platform you choose to work with, you have the foundation locked in for a strong strategy that will earn you growth and, more importantly, profits.

How Social Media Works For Business
The purpose of social media for general users is fairly straightforward: you get on your chosen platform and begin to network with your friends and family. If you are looking to grow your network, you can add other people who are interested in similar things as you are and then become "digital friends" with them. In other words, you never actually meet them in person, but you share with them online on a consistent basis and get to know them through status updates, comments, and other social media conversations. It truly is about networking and, more importantly, talking and sharing with one another.
This is exactly what makes social media such a powerful platform for businesses to market their products on.
It has long been known that word of mouth is one of the most powerful marketing strategies at the disposal of any company. If you want to grow your business, having people share positive comments and experiences about your business while recommending you to others is a great way to start.
Meanwhile, if they are sharing negative comments or bad experiences, that is a great way to end up running out of clients because people stop trusting you and, therefore, stop doing business with you. If you want to have success, then, you need to earn the positive comments and recommendations from people who have fallen in love with your business.

Since social media is already all about talking, sharing, and networking with others, it makes sense that this is an incredibly powerful platform to get on when it comes to marketing your business. People are already leveraging word of mouth; all you need to do is get on there and give them something to talk about. By creating a profile for your business and sharing content on a regular basis, you give people plenty to talk about through your profile. This way, all they need to do is engage with your business and share with others so that you are being seen by those who are most likely to purchase from you.

Because of the power of social media and the power of word of mouth, an incredible modern business has evolved from this system. That is: influencers. Becoming an influencer means taking on a business model where you are at the center of conversations, and you are the one influencing what people are talking about. Essentially, becoming an influencer means that you build your popularity on social media and then begin talking about products or services that you love, thus causing those who follow you to talk about them, too. Because you are popular and they already trust you, they are more likely to purchase these products or services.

Becoming an influencer gives you the opportunity to charge businesses for your endorsement, essentially meaning that you are paid a commission every time someone purchases something because you influenced them to. As a result, you can earn money solely through becoming popular on social media and then guiding people to purchase certain products or services through companies that are willing to pay you.

Both starting your own business giving something people to talk about or running a business where you influence people to talk about certain things, are great ways to get involved in social media marketing so that you can make a profit online. In this book, we are going to talk about how you can conquer both of these models online, allowing you to build the online business empire of your dreams, no matter what that might look like.

Choosing The Right Niche On Social Media

The first thing that you need to do when you begin to leverage social media for growing a business is find out what your niche is. A niche outlines a specific segment of your chosen industry that you are going to talk to, which is necessary if you are going to make an impact in social media marketing. Because billions of people use social media every month, and most industries are marketing to multiple millions of people, you need to have a specific segment of the market that you are talking to if you are going to be heard. Otherwise, people are going to ignore you because your information and updates do not feel personable enough for them to really relate with, connect to, and pay attention to you.

Choosing the right niche on social media is necessary regardless of where you are at in business or what business model you are using to make money online. However, there will be certain steps that you need to adjust if you are going to be developing a business online to ensure that you are choosing the niche that is going to give you the most opportunity to grow online.

If you already have a business that you have been running off of social media, choosing the right niche on social media is about finding the part of your audience that is most likely to pay attention to you in the online space. So, if your market is generally 30-40 year old women in person, you need to find out which types of women you are marketing to the most and who is spending the most time online, and then you need to focus your marketing efforts on them.

With a business already up and running, targeting your niche online is going to be incredibly simple because you already have statistics available to show you who pays the most attention to your marketing, and to your business in general. All you need to do is refine these statistics to identify who is online and what they are talking about so that you can find the right angle to talk with them online.

For example, Horace and Jasper is a leather company located in Calgary, Alberta. Their company creates belts, purses, bags, wallets, cellphone charms, wrist cuffs, and more. In reality, this company could market to just about anyone who would wear a belt or carry a wallet because of how versatile their products are. However, if they were to market to just anyone, they would not have any success in getting discovered online. Instead, they have decided to market specifically to edgy, punk rock type that is looking to shop local for products that are higher quality and backed with a more trustworthy guarantee. This way, they are speaking to a very specific segment of their possible market, which results in a massive amount of success in their marketing strategies and business growth.

Another great example of how this works is with the Honest Company. This company provides baby care and cleaning products that are cleaner, more environmentally friendly, and less harmful to your family. Ideally, they could market to anyone who lives in a house or who has young children because they are providing products that are relevant to these two segments of the market. However, they know that the people most likely to purchase their products are women who are environmentally conscious and who want to do better for their families. So, they tend to market toward women and moms who are wanting a safer alternative to harsh chemicals, which results in them having massive growth on their online platform, as well as their business in general.

Identifying your niche is less about paring down and finding one single type of person to talk to, and more about identifying the angle that you use on social media. You want to find the angle that is going to give you a specific way to talk to and share with your audience so that the ones who are most likely to purchase through you are listening and purchasing.

This is true for anyone who is just starting out in business, too. If you are starting a business with the purpose of generating success online, or if you are becoming an influencer, you are going to need to find a niche so that you know who you are talking to, why, and how to reach them. This way, you are more likely to reach those individuals.

As someone who does not already have a business in place, you do face the setback of not already having statistics around who you are most likely to earn sales from, which means that you are going to have to start from scratch. However, starting fresh means that you do have the capacity to choose the niche that is most interesting to you while also having the most growth potential online, which can be an incredible opportunity to maximize your success.

If you are brand new in business, the best thing that you can do is determine what type of business model you want to follow, and then research what the latest trends are in that particular model. So, if you want to sell products or services, you need to identify what types of products or services are selling the most online. If you want to be an influencer, you need to identify what types of influencers are making the most income online. The key here is to make sure that you are looking at the right numbers. Avoid looking at industries that have the most businesses that are online, and instead look at the industries that have the most businesses that are actually making a strong profit online. This is how you can ensure that you are choosing a niche that is going to be lucrative in offering you great opportunities to make money, rather than choosing a niche that is going to be saturated with businesses or influencers. If it is saturated and no one is making a decent profit, there is a good chance that you are looking at a low quality industry.

While you look at industries that are going to offer the most opportunity, make sure that you are also looking for industries that are interesting to you. Attempting to make a go at it in an industry that you do not understand or that does not interest you is going to end with you falling flat because you are not passionate enough to really give it the type of energy it needs to grow. Instead, pick one that makes you excited because that will make it far easier to help you gain the momentum that you need to grow your business rapidly and have great success with it, too.

Chapter 2: Finding the Right Platforms for your Brand

Throughout this guide, we will look into various options for social media sites that are useful for your marketing needs. You will become an expert on the various social media platforms and which of them might be most effective for your business. This can also vary depending on what your marketing goals are for a particular campaign. For example, if your goal is brand recognition one platform might be better, if your goal is brand loyalty, you might take a different approach with a different platform. Etc.

Naturally, you can always work with all social media sites we list here; as many as you want to make yourself visible. Nevertheless, that does not mean every single one of them is sensible for your needs, let alone easy to use.

Every social media site is different based on whom it targets and how it is organized. Each social media site is unique.

Choose carefully when planning your social media campaign. If anything, having multiple social media sites is best as it gives you the opportunity to accomplish more.

This chapter looks into individual social media sites and how you should evaluate them.

Look at the main goals you have for a social media campaign. Decide why you are choosing social media in the first place. Maybe you want people to be more aware of your brand. Perhaps you are just trying to get more leads. Perhaps you might be trying to get people to download an app or reach your physical place of business.

The social media space you visit should be chosen based on what your goals are. Facebook is ideal if you want people to be more aware of your work. LinkedIn is perfect if you want to get leads. Snapchat is ideal if you want people to download an app.

Whatever the case, look at what you can get out of a social media site before you start working with it. See that the campaign is arranged correctly and that you have a clear understanding what social media sites are perfect for it. You should carefully examine how individual options might work with your various needs.

Consider the target audience you are trying to reach.

Every social media site has its own specific audience. LinkedIn has a great platform that is popular among professionals, especially those who earn good wages. Instagram is useful for younger people and is prominent among today's millennials. In 2015, the Pew Research Center found some interesting demographics surrounding social media sites. While this information is not definitive, it provides an idea of what to expect from certain social media sites:

•   Facebook's user-base is extremely diverse. People of all kinds use Facebook - from the rich and poor to the young and old alike. It is equally popular among men and women and among black, white, Hispanic, and Asian audiences and other racial demographics.

•   Women are more interested in using Pinterest. People from suburban areas are also interested in it more than others.

•   LinkedIn is not only popular with wealthier people but also with those who have college degrees. People living in urban areas tend to use LinkedIn more often too.

•   Younger people are more likely to use Twitter. Those living in urban areas will use it more often as well.

This is just a sampling of what you will discover about social media sites. All of these sites are different in how they attract various types of people. Experiment with different social media pages so you can potentially get something meaningful and important out of your campaign. As you will discover, be watchful how you can use multiple options for your campaign. Look at how often people might interact with social media sites.

All social media sites have different standards of how often people interact with them. Facebook, Twitter, and Instagram are the most popular places where people are more likely to check every day or every other day. Meanwhile, Pinterest and LinkedIn are places where people will check on their feeds three to five times a week although some might do that more often.

A site that has people checking it often if you are trying to increase your brand recognition might be advisable. Sites where people do not check their profiles every day are good if you are trying to get leads or establish long-term connections with professionals in a field.

Knowing how people behave on social media sites is important when you want to interact with them. Make sure you find out how well and how easy you can communicate with someone on a site. This is to make it easier for you to interact with people and to share your interests.

Review what your competitors are doing.

Your competition will more than likely be on social media already or contemplating joining in the future. Whatever the case might be, look at what your competitors are doing.

Check the websites of your challengers to see what others are doing. Be sure to do what you can to compete with them and of course make sure your approach focuses on your competitive edge and what you offer that your competitors do not offer. Doing so makes it easier for your page to stand out and be more attractive. Monitor the performance of your campaign and continuously tweak and adjust until you feel that your message is clear and well received. It's also important to make sure you are not copying whatever other people are doing. Using the same social media sites and working with similar keywords or other posting strategies is good so long as your content is original.

You do not necessarily have to duplicate everything your opponents do. Be aware of what someone else is implementing so you have a clear idea of what you should do yourself. Keep your mind open throughout the process, but at least examine the accomplishments of others.

Think about the content you want to create.

Every social media site is different in terms of the message you work with. You can do anything on a social media page, but you need to discover what the standards are for each site:

• Tumblr, Pinterest, Snapchat, and Instagram are great if you are trying to market things with pictures. These social media sites are perfect for pictorial-based marketing.

• LinkedIn is ideal if you want to be more technical. The site is also great for people who want to share their opinions with others.

• YouTube and Snapchat are good for video content.

• Quora is appealing if you want to answer questions that people might have about a certain concept your business has.

• Twitter is useful for when you want to share news or ideas with people. Although only if you are trying to share smaller bits of data at a time.

Review the context before you choose a certain social media site. This is all about getting some control over your work and having everything laid out in a smart and valuable manner. As you practice, you'll improve your ability to do this and your customers will catch on.

Look at the format of your content.

All social media sites have standards for how the content is posted. YouTube obviously focuses on videos while Instagram is about pictures. Twitter is for smaller messages while Facebook and LinkedIn allow more details about what you want to post.

Decide on what to post and how it will be illustrated. This is to give you a better approach to handle your work.

Think about the subject you will utilize as well. Some businesses might work better with specific types of content. A tax preparation firm might do best with blog posts explaining changes in tax laws, for instance. A baseball training facility could benefit from having video posts showing people learning how to play the game or honing their skills.

Be careful when launching your campaigns:

Don't run too many social media campaigns. Know how well you can handle individual ones without getting overwhelmed. While you can work with as many social media sites as you want, only commit to what you are comfortable with handling at any given time. You do not want to forget about individual sites. In this respect, quality is more important than quantity. It's better to have one excellent campaign than 5 mediocre ones. Moreover, your customer will be annoyed if they are constantly being plagues by mediocre ads and campaigns. They will lose interest in your brand.

You can always use the analytical features from many social media sites to see what is happening with your pages. Analytics examine how many visitors reach your site or interact with your posts. You can use analytics to assess the progress of paid campaigns you operate. This research will help you determine whether to stay with a particular platform or if you are better off elsewhere. Do not use anything too complicated or hard to follow because after all, your workload will get more difficult.

If needed, there is also the option to network with others in your business to work with different campaigns. You could hire one person to run a Facebook campaign while another works on LinkedIn, for instance. See how well those people handle individual campaigns and if they understand how certain social media platforms work. Allow multiple people to work with several channels at a time if you have to, but see that they understand what they are working with. The key is to keep everything in your social media campaign consistent and under control.

Remember that all the points introduced in this chapter are mere suggestions. You could always work with any of the social media sites you are reading about in this guide. Consider what each of these sites has to offer so you can do more with your work.

Chapter 3: Facebook Marketing

One of the longest standing platforms out there to date is Facebook. Facebook came around in 2004 and has continued to grow in popularity ever since. Over the years, the company has shifted its platform to serve both personal connections and professional connections so that people can use it either for personal use or business use. For that reason, Facebook has also become one of the most popular platforms for marketing your business on.

These days, Facebook offers many excellent features for people who are wanting to promote their business online. In an effort to diversify their platform and create more equal opportunities for business owners, while also keeping the platform enjoyable for personal use, Facebook has introduced features such as business pages, promotional opportunities, and groups. You can use all of these to market yourself or your brand on Facebook.

Who Should Use Facebook, And Why?
When it comes to getting your business online, everyone needs to be on Facebook in one way or another. Due to the way that this platform is designed, as well as the reputation that it has built for itself, everyone can benefit from having their business on Facebook. These days, people are more likely to search Facebook or Instagram for your business than they are Google, as they want to see what type of image you are maintaining with your business. Finding you on a social media platform gives your followers a greater opportunity to not only find basic information about your business, but also more personalized information about your business. More importantly, they are going to identify whether or not you are reliable, and if they are a part of your target audience.

Creating a Facebook page will ensure that if anyone turns to Facebook to look you up, they can find you. This means that you also need to maintain your page in a way that is going to give them something to look at and develop an opinion from right away, rather than having a page that is just as plain as Google's results page.

If you are using Facebook just to create a landing page, you are going to want to post at least once per week to ensure that the page looks up to date and has enough content on it to show your audience who you are. This way, people do not get the idea that your brand is inactive or inconsistent, which could lead to them not trusting in your business or losing interest relatively quickly. That being said, you can use it to turn your audience to another platform as well, allowing you to get even more viewers onto a platform that you are actually using.

If you want to use Facebook as one of your primary platforms, you can do that as well. The only difference will be that you are going to update your page more frequently so that there is plenty of new content for people to find. You may also wish to use other platforms to encourage people to land on your Facebook page, helping you to funnel more possible followers to your platform.

Leveraging Facebook In Your Marketing Strategy

As I have recently mentioned, the two best ways to leverage Facebook into your marketing strategy is to either use it as a primary platform to connect with your followers, or design it to be a landing page that funnels people to another platform. These are very basic ways to take advantage of Facebook and its reputation to reach your audience.

There are other ways that you can leverage Facebook in your marketing strategy in 2020 as well, however. These ways are going to give you the best opportunity to develop your online presence and grow your Facebook page with ease.

In the past, the best way to use your page was to simply add a profile picture and some words about your business and then update your status fairly regularly. These days, however, it works differently. One of the best ways to leverage Facebook as a part of your marketing strategy in 2020 is to use it as a platform to share your products and services with others. You can do this by completely filling out every single part of your Facebook page with information about who you are, what your business is all about, what products and services you have to offer, and where you can be located. You can even sell your products and services right there on Facebook, or offer a booking feature so that people can book a service with your company.

The amount of features that are available on Facebook is massive, making it an excellent platform for people who want to sell their products. In fact, many marketing agencies are now saying that smaller businesses can run their entire online business exclusively through Facebook without the need of a website or another platform to sell anything on. This is actually a great way of putting everything online without having to spend quite as much to maintain a website and a purchasing platform.

As you learn to work Facebook into your marketing strategy, your best opportunity is to turn it either into a "hub" of sorts where people can go to do business with you. This can either be the hub that people land on after interacting with one of your more engaged platforms like Instagram or Twitter, or it can be the primary hub where people go to engage with your business in any way that they desire. You can decide how much or how little you want to be active on Facebook, but the key to making Facebook work for you is actually getting on it and creating some form of strong presence there.

Marketing On Facebook In 2020

If you want to come off on top with your Facebook marketing strategy for 2020, you are going to have to take yourself beyond the basics and really learn how to work your page. The best way to do that is to get on Facebook and get yourself acquainted with the different tabs and different features available to you as a business owner so that you know exactly what you can do to set your page up for success.

Just like in the previous years, you are going to need to create your page with a branded page name, a branded profile picture and cover image, and a custom description. You should also customize your page's username, which can be done by going to the desktop version of your browser and tapping on the "Create Page @username" under your page name. The username that you use here should be the exact same username that you are going to user on other platforms so that everyone who looks for your page knows what to look for across all platforms.

Once you have set up the basics, you can begin to customize your page. You can start this process by going to the "Settings" part of your page and then tapping "Templates and Tabs." There, you are going to get the opportunity to choose what type of page you want to have, and what customizable features you want access to on your page. In terms of templates, Facebook offers ten template options: standard, video page, shopping, restaurants & cafes, services, politicians, nonprofit, venues, business, and movies. You want to pick the one that is relevant to your business, as this is going to give you the best tab features relating to your business model.

Once you have chosen your template, you can begin to customize your tabs, or the features available on your business page. The tabs that you will have access to for customization features will depend on which template you have chosen, however you can add or remove tabs to your template by scrolling to the bottom of the Templates & Tabs page and clicking "Add A Tab." If you want to remove a tab, you can click "Settings" next to that tab and select "Delete." You can easily re-add any tab you delete, but you may need to revise it to feature all of your business' information once again. You can also rearrange the order of the tabs by clicking on the three grey lines to the left side of each tab and then dragging them into your desired order.

After you have created your template and chosen your tabs, you will need to go back to the main view of your page in order to begin customizing each tab. From there, tap the tab that you want to customize and then select "edit" next to any feature that you want to change. You will then be walked through the process of adjusting the information in that given tab so that it reflects what you need for your business.

When you are customizing your tabs, make sure that you are considering what your customer's experience is going to be like when they land on your page. You want to make sure that it is easy to navigate, and that it is easy to find any relevant information that they may need when it comes time for them to buy through you. This means that your pictures need to be more than just an extremely basic corporate-type photograph, and your descriptions need to be more customized as well. You want to make sure that as your customer browses your page to find information it is easy for them to find it, whether that is about products they can buy through your page, services they can book through your page, or other platforms they can find you on. The more thoughtful your presentation is, the easier it is going to be for people to find what they are looking for on your page so that they can get what they want and carry on. With online shopping, convenience and appearance is everything.

Once you have customized a tab, go back to your main page and browse that tab as if you were a stranger to your page. Get a feel for how it is to navigate that tab, whether or not you can easily find what you are looking for, and if you impressed by the overall appearance and functionality of that tab. If you are not, consider making the necessary revisions so that you can make your page more attractive and functional.

Chapter 4: Instagram Marketing

As you may already know by now, Instagram is a social media website which lets its users edit, filter and share pictures and videos to many other people over the Internet. It also allows users to simultaneously share these over Twitter, Facebook, Flickr and Tumblr. According to statisticbrain.com, Instagram has over 183 million registered users who have already shared more than 18 billion pictures and videos that garner an average of 1.65 billion likes daily as of 11 September 2015. If that's not big enough for you, I don't know what is! Businesses have also started looking to Instagram to sell their brands, particularly because pictures (and videos) paint a thousand (and more) words, and our brains think better in pictures.   These major businesses include G.E., Adidas, Virgin America, American Express, Intel and Red Bull, among many others. In reality, almost every major business out there has some type of Instagram presence, but many do not take full advantage of the platform or execute a good marketing strategy with Instagram.

Intel, for example, promotes their latest, cutting-edge processors via Instagram with pictures of the latest computer models that utilize them. More than just posting pictures on Instagram, they post highly creative pictures that make their otherwise "boring" products come to life with excitement. It features all sorts of technological wonders on its Instagram, including both widely available products as well as more eccentric but rapidly growing choices like 3-D printers. Its Instagram account features a wide range of photos that paint different pictures as to how Intel's products continue to influence our way of life as we know it.

In contrast, the Instagram account of Virgin America is less creatively styled than most others. At one point, they used photos of the very popular Pomeranian puppy Boo in promoting their first class flights as dog-friendly over this social media site.

American Express promotes its financial services on Instagram, particularly by posting mostly photos of the many important events they've sponsored as well as by using #hashtags in promoting their products' image as those that are essential for modern living.

Keep in mind that while you can post short videos on Instagram, it's not optimal to do so. If you're gunning for video promotions, your best bet is still YouTube, which is designed primarily for uploading videos. Focus your resources on beautifully creative pictures and images on Instagram to optimize your use of this particular social media platform.

Posting pics on Instagram isn't as easy as snapping photos and uploading them – at least not for social media marketing purposes. Before you promote your products or services of this social media platform, consider your target audience, the optimal engagement strategy and what will provoke them into talking about your brand and photographs. When you know your audience well, you'll know the kinds of pictures that'll appeal to them. Instagram allows you to get truly creative with your marketing, enabling you to use it to advertise virtually any product. Once you get to know your customer base, design a beautifully well-pictured marketing campaign that will appeal to the audience you are trying to attract. When you know your audience well, you'll also be able to develop strategies that will get them to talk about your brand, which provides opportunities for engagement and consequently, brand awareness and promotion.

BEST PRACTICES

By also posting pictures of the people behind your products and services on Instagram, you "humanize" your business by allowing your followers to see the hands and faces behind the inanimate objects they are following on Instagram. Social media in all of its many forms depends, primarily, on connecting with our fellow human beings. Let your potential customers see you as you work, and witness the hands-on, emotional, relatable side of your business, as opposed to just the end result they so commonly see. Humanizing your products and services allows your followers to connect with your business on a deeper level and increases their chances of becoming hot leads and eventually, customers.

You can also draw in more prospects and leads by featuring pictures that show how your products are created and packaged or how your services are rendered. The point of doing this is to make your followers more familiar with your brand so they can become leads and customers. If they understand more of how your process works from the start, they are more likely to trust and rely on your products and in doing so, they will come to rely on your business as well.

Most people are naturally curious and knowing what goes into the creation of items they enjoy can make them feel more attached to such items, as well as offering them reassurance that the methods you claim to use are every bit as ethical as you suggest, gaining you additional trust and loyalty. Just don't give too much "detail" to prevent your competition from spying on you and undercutting you.

Lastly, use original unique and catchy #hashtags, Instagram's most effective marketing tactic. Using good hashtags can help your brand become more visible to more people, which can lead to more prospects, leads and consequently sales. You want a good mix of unique hashtags with more popular hashtags. To evaluate the popularity of a particular hashtag, all you have to do is type it into the search box on Instagram and you'll see how many other posts are currently using that same hashtag.

Chapter 5: Youtube Marketing

Google owns this platform that allows its users to upload, share, comment on and watch videos. Its search engine is probably the 2nd biggest in the world next to its parent company and by far, the biggest video sharing website on the planet. As such, it's the best social media platform to use videos in promoting your products and services. But with so many videos being uploaded on YouTube – about 72 hours' worth of video every minute being uploaded on the site – how can you effectively reach your target audiences?

The first thing you'll need to do is create your own "channel" on YouTube, which should neither be too difficult nor complicated. Next, comes the most challenging part, producing very compelling videos for upload.

So what makes for compelling videos? First, consider the content, which should engage your target customers within 15 seconds or less. Otherwise, your viewers will be bored and won't bother watching your videos long enough to appreciate it. This is because of the information overload they're all subject to each and every day. To really engage them within the first 15 seconds, use introductions that are animated and quick to both spark their curiosity and win their trust. This helps them expect something great from watching the video further.

Another important quality your videos need to have are calls to action – and this is key for any social media campaign to succeed. You can place the call to action at any point on the video, depending of course on its message. Just ensure you don't overdo your calls to action because for one, having too many such calls may confuse the viewers or it may come across as aggressive or pushy. After all, much like Facebook, people are not on youtube to buy things. They're there to either find information or else be entertained. So you need to make sure whatever content you provide checks one or both of those boxes (hopefully both).

Some of the common and sensible calls to action you can consider including in your videos are subscribing to your YouTube channel, commenting on your videos, liking-adding-sharing your videos and visiting your brand's official website and/or other social media platforms, among others. These are less aggressive asks. This doesn't cost the viewer anything and if they feel connected to you and inspired by your content, they may well want to support you or at least they want to hear more of what you have to say.

And more than just compelling, you should also post videos on YouTube regularly to increase your presence in YouTube and consequently, increase the number of your subscribers. One way to ensure regularity is to create shorter videos of a particular long-form content, i.e., divide one long topic or video into series of shorter videos. Instead of producing a "movie", create shorter episodes that are not only easier to watch and understand but also spark more curiosity and interest. It can help if you release each new segment on a designated day and time, and remain consistent.

Once you get people hooked on your channel, they'll be eagerly looking forward to watching your new video each time a new one is posted, and if you let them know when that will be, they'll incorporate your channel into part of their daily routine. Be careful to avoid sporadic or infrequent updates, though, or your followers are likely to grow bored and no longer anticipate content, leading to less loyalty and fewer customers. Be consistent, and make it entertaining, and your current clients will recommend your videos to their friends, likely via social media itself.

Video Visibility

No amount of consistency in terms of posting high-quality and interesting videos on YouTube will ever make up for lack of visibility. After all, what good are videos – however excellent the content – if viewers can't find them? While this is more about search engine optimization (SEO), which is a very complicated topic to discuss here, you can do the following to improve your videos' visibility and allow more people to view it.

One is carefully written titles. Make sure that your videos' titles include targeted keywords and that they're followed by a colon (:) for optimal visibility.

Next are your videos' descriptions, which you'll need to begin with a full URL. You'll also need to provide as many details about the video as possible without giving away its main attractions or points so that people will still want to watch it. In other words, enough details without spoilers.

Chapter 6: Twitter Marketing

Twitter has been a highly controversial platform in the past, with many claiming that it is becoming "irrelevant" or that it is too challenging for smaller businesses to use. Some have even gone so far as to claim that Twitter is not ideal for certain industries, discriminating against companies that have younger, older, or more eclectic audiences than the average company. In fact, a common myth that was passed around for much of 2018-2019 is that Twitter is only beneficial if you are a politician or a white collar business person. Many believed that its sole focuses were stocks, politics, business, and relevant news articles.

Believe it or not: none of this is true, and knowing this may just make Twitter your best tool for growth in 2020.

Twitter has actually been proven to be one of the most effective platforms for businesses to get on, offering a whopping 80% click-through rate, where 80% of visitors on your profile are actually going and visiting your URL, too. People on Twitter are highly active, love to check out new businesses, and believe that if a business is on Twitter, it is a business worth knowing about. In fact, in 2019 a study showed that 85% of Twitter users said that they believe it is crucial that a business is on Twitter, particularly so that they can offer customer support. Clearly, Twitter is an incredible tool for business, no matter how large, small, or niche your business may be.

Leveraging Twitter In Your Marketing Strategy

The marketing strategy that you use on Twitter is going to largely depend on how big your business is and who your audience is. Unlike Instagram which relies largely on topics and trending hashtags, Twitter actually also relies on proximity as a valuable tool in helping you grow your audience and increase your impact. By using proximity, you can leverage the power of local, national, or global audiences to grow your platform and get found. The key is knowing what size your business is, who your audience is, and who is going to be the most likely to care at each point in your platforms growth.

If you are a smaller business, or you are just starting out, you want to focus on a close proximity to you. Getting on Twitter and targeting local trends is a great way for you to begin to get found on the Twitter platform, as this way you are not attempting to target too large of an audience. When you target local trends and local groups of people, you give yourself a greater opportunity to get found because you are not competing against so many people who are trying to speak to the same audience as you are. Whereas a larger business with a bigger name may have an easier time getting found in the larger audiences, you as a smaller business and with a smaller reputation will have a hard time. This is truly the key to getting your foot in the door.

As your audience begins to grow and your business begins to grow as well, you can start targeting larger audiences. You can do this by looking into your national audience and targeting national trends. Although smaller businesses can do this too, you should avoid doing it too frequently as a smaller business to avoid being drown out by the rest of the people speaking to your audience. Alternatively, as a smaller business or a transitioning business you can combine national and local trends to improve your odds of being seen by your target audience.

Once your business begins to get larger and more well-known, you can start targeting international and global trends. This way, you have a larger built-in audience that is already going to be communicating with you through their timelines, which will actually improve your odds of being seen in the trending topics by people outside of your existing audience. Using this approach will help you grow even larger so that you can get found by a greater number of people, allowing your business to grow even faster. If you are a small or medium business, or if you have a small or medium audience on Twitter, you can still use global trends but you should avoid using them as your primary focus. Instead, either use them from time to time while focusing primarily on your local or national audience, or use them in addition to a local and national audience in a single post to increase your chances of getting seen.

Speaking to the right size of an audience on Twitter is crucial, as this is how you are really going to get found online. Again, attempting to speak to too large of an audience when you do not have a strong enough reputation or recognition to support you is only going to cause your brand to get drown out amongst all of the other voices. Really knowing how big of an audience you can reasonably speak to is crucial in helping you get the word out there and grow your platform more rapidly. As you begin to grow your business, you can begin to grow your reach, too, allowing you to get even further out there.

If you are a business that deals primarily with a certain audience, such as a local business that deals primarily with local people, or a global business that deals primarily with global people, following the aforementioned strategy is still important for you. Even though you might not be targeting your exact audience at all points, you will be growing your popularity and visibility which means that your target audience will be more likely to see you. The larger audience, even if it is outside of your typical sales audience, will increase your perceived value, making you more likely to sell products or services while also making it easier for you to sell your products or services at a higher price tag. This way, you can leverage your audience for improved profits, not just for improved visibility and discoverability.

Marketing On Twitter In 2020

When it comes to marketing on Twitter in 2020, you are going to want to first identify the size of your existing audience. If you are brand new on Twitter, chances are you do not have a very large audience and so you are going to need to start off targeting smaller audiences. If you have been on Twitter for some time and you are looking to upgrade your strategy, you may already have a fairly decent sized audience. For the purpose of this book, we are going to group Twitter audience sizes accordingly: small audiences are any audience with 0-5000 followers, medium audiences are any audience with 5,000 – 15,000 followers, and large audiences are anyone with 15,000+ followers. This counts for organic, active followers, and not followers that were purchased through a platform like Fiverr or Upwork. Once you have identified where your audience size lies, you can begin applying the following techniques for marketing with your Twitter account in 2020. First, you are going to want to modernize the branding on your profile. In 2018, branding was largely centered around an incredibly clean and polished appearance, complete with stock images or images that looked like stock images. These photographs were created to give a clean, professional, and modern look into what your company offered or represented, and was said to be appealing to the eye. This is, in fact, true, and supported many businesses in growing through 2018 and 2019. That being said, trends are changing for 2020. Studies have shown that the number of brands misusing stock images to create low-quality high-profit brands online have grown, causing consumers to become wary when they profiles filled with stock images or overly polished photographs. Although they do want to see images that are high quality and professional, more and more people are wanting to get away from the stock image appearance and start seeing something more personal, artistic, and inspirational.

As you create the imagery for your profile, you are going to need to create with the idea of being more personable in mind. You want your profile to have character, to represent a brand that stands apart from the generic click-and-build brands of 2018 and 2019, and to be worthy of earning people's attention so that they decide to follow you and engage with your content. This means that your pictures should continue to be high quality and with a clear focal point, but that they should be personalized to feature characteristics that are representative of your brand. Furthermore, these characteristics should be high quality and artistic in a sense. If you are not the artistic type, a quick browse around other Twitter profiles can help give you an idea of how other people are customizing their profiles, simply pay closer attention to the ones that are more personalized and authentic.

On Twitter, the focus is less on graphics and more on verbal marketing, so you have less space for your images on your profile. That being said, avoid having "busy" images which are going to take away from the quality of your profile. Attempting to be artistic whilst creating images that are too busy for your audience to really know what they are looking at is actually going to minimize the quality of your profile, and therefore the number of people who find you and follow you. Instead, find a way to be artistic while using details sparingly in your images. For example, if you are a clothing designer, rather than having a picture of you posed in front of clothing racks, which would look incredibly busy in a small image, have a picture of you posed in front of a store window wearing the clothes that you designed. This way, you are able to show off your character without overwhelming the image and making it difficult for your audience to really know what they are looking at.

In addition to your graphics, you need to brand your bio and your link. Again, roughly 80% of the people who land on your page are going to visit your link, so having a relevant and high quality link that leads people directly to an opportunity to purchase or work with you is important. This way, you can take advantage of those 80% of people and drive more traffic to your website, another platform, or an affiliate link where you are going to earn more money than you might on Twitter.

Creating your bio on Twitter in 2020 needs to be simple, and filled with personality. One liners are still incredibly popular, with brands creating a single sentence that summarizes their entire brand, including its personality, in just a few words. You can also add an additional sentence to discuss any upcoming points of interest that you may have to share with your audience. For example: "Take your cheese habit to the next level with unusual and unique cheese flavors. New flavors launching 05/10." Remember that you only have 160 characters to write out your bio, so you need to choose something that packs a punch and gets the message across as quickly as possible. This way, people get an immediate feel for who you are, what your brand represents, and what they can expect to find on your page. When you are done, add a link to your bio area so that people can find that, as well.

The next way to leverage Twitter for marketing in 2020 is to pay close attention to the trends. Twitter is one of the most well-known platforms for spotting and following trends online, as it has an entire page catered toward highlighting trending topics that are collected from the platform itself, as well as news platforms and gossip columns. Using Twitter specifically to learn about trending topics is a great opportunity for you to grow your platform, while also gaining insight into how you can grow on other platforms, too. This way, you can stay relevant and your audience is more likely to keep up with you and pay attention to what you are posting.

Remember, you want to focus on trends and topics based on what proximity is going to be most reasonable for your audience size. If you have a smaller audience, look to find the trends that are currently growing in your local area so that you can get on board with talking about those trends, or even incorporating them into your products, services, or sales. For example, if you have a local celebration going on that celebrates something in specific, you might consider creating products, services, or even a special sale to celebrate with your local area. This is a great opportunity to get more local eyes on you, helping you expand your reach and grow your audience. If you have a medium sized business, focus on national trends, and if you have a large sized business, focus on global trends. Continue paying close attention to the trends relevant to your business size, while also playing around with trends that cater to other audience sizes from time to time, too. This way, you are always marketing toward an audience that is going to be large enough for you to grow in, but small enough for you to get found in.

Chapter 7: Rapidly Scale Your Business Step By Step In Social Media

Before you jump into social media marketing in these time, it's imperative that you know the basic outlines of the process of brand building through social media platforms and SEO. In this section of the book, we will cover the basics on how to approach brand building in a structural manner before actually starting to work on building your social media presence and website to create your own identifiable brand. Necessity in Today's World

From now on, it will no longer be possible to create a memorable personal branding by pulling wild-child antics like Richard Branson once did in the 80s and 90s; Elon Musk is living proof of this fact. To build a brand successfully in today's world, you need to utilize internet marketing, which is mostly a combination of social media marketing and SEO. Some digital marketing professionals might swear by SEO and quality content as the pillars of modern-day brand building, but it's foolish to ignore the power of social media and the kind of exposure it can bring to your brand. Inbound marketing from search engines is definitely a crucial aspect of brand building, but to get people searching for your brand on Google or YouTube, your content needs to be exposed first on social media - namely Facebook and Instagram, two of the most powerful and most used social media platforms in the world. With around 2.5 billion users worldwide, the reach of social media is unlike anything else that can be used to promote a brand. Although, this may be the best way to build your brand, do not expect it to be easy or rewarded in a short time. Just like every other famous and successful brand, it takes effort and time to grow. The best example of a brand using social media to build itself is Daniel Wellington. Founded in 2011, Daniel Wellington is a Swedish watch company that took full advantage of social media marketing, so much so that it was included in the top ten fastest growing companies in all of Europe. Although Daniel Wellington did not have a rich history behind it like other big watch brands, it used the power of proper marketing to position itself among the populous and grab a huge portion of the market.
SWOT Analysis

To judge if a strategy is suitable or not, it is necessary to learn about everything that the strategy has to offer. This is where SWOT analysis of a strategy comes in. SWOT is basically analyzing the strength, weakness, opportunity, and threat of a strategy, hence the name. The strength and weaknesses are what inherently come with the strategy, and the opportunities and threat are what the target market brings forward. Let us take a look at the SWOT analysis for branding via social media so that we can weigh the good against the bad and see if this is actually the right approach.

Strength: The goal of social media is simple - to connect people. This goal has been achieved and more. Log into any of the popular social media sites, and you will get to meet or see people of all races, genders, ethnicities, financial statuses, and from all locations. So, the strength of social media marketing is pretty obvious, and that is reach. Social media will allow you to reach people from all walks of life, thus giving you the opportunity to target a very big market. If you can take advantage of this strength, then you can have a huge following in no time, which is what makes this strategy so lucrative.

Weakness: As with all strategies, social media marketing also has its share of weakness. Among others, the one that stands out the most is also related to the strength it provides. You see that though you will be able to reach a lot of people with SMM strategy, you will not be able to control the type of people that view your content fully. You may be able to target specific audiences through segmenting, but even among them, there may be ones that may not take a liking to your content. This means you are open to more criticism than that you might have faced using other methods. However, this weakness can easily be overcome by constantly trying to improve your brand and taking feedback. Also, you will also have to remember that you cannot satisfy everyone at the same time, so when facing any outliers, you cannot take the things they say or their actions to heart and let them discourage you.

Opportunity: Although you will be presented with a lot of opportunities right from the market, the most important one will be when your brand starts to grow. During this time, you will be given the opportunity to understand the market in even more detail and most importantly, build a network. In any marketing strategy, networking is an absolute must to further grow your brand. Once your business starts to grow, you will be exposed to other brands and influencers big and small. If you can work your way to their good side, then your network will start to grow dramatically and without much effort, so make sure to grab this opportunity when it appears.

Threats: The threats that the market will present to you are common across all types of strategies. So, even if you were to take a different approach, you would come across these threats at one point or another. However, the difference when using social media branding is that you will be exposed to these threats on a bigger scale. For example, once your brand starts to become successful, you might start to face competition in the form of other brands copying your ideas. They might bring slight changes to your idea to take over a certain portion of your market. No matter, though, you can easily overcome threats by being spontaneous. You must always keep yourself updated with the changes in the market and prepare instant countermeasures if any of those changes pose a threat to your brand.

After taking a look at all these factors, it is pretty clear that social media marketing is the best way to market your brand at present, since it will provide more opportunities than other methods and has weaknesses that can be easily overcome.

Developing Assets

Now that you know the effectiveness of social media marketing let's dive right into how to build your own brand through social media.

Brand goals

The first step to building a brand is to properly define it. Do you want to build a brand that is unique and meant for a niche market, or do you want to set yourself apart using unique marketing and prices? Whatever your answer may be, it is very important that you are sure about your brand goal, since your brand and everything related to it will be based on this moving forward.

Something that will help you define your brand goal is understanding your expertise. You should always base your brand on things that you are good at or things that you have a passion for. If you are in it only for the money, then you will quickly lose interest in your brand which will be quite visible to your target market. So, it is important that you understand what your strength is and use that to your advantage while building a brand. Examples of people building their brand around their expertise can be seen everywhere, from beauty brands to Tesla which was built around Elon's Musk ability to come up with new and revolutionary ideas.

Brand strategy

Once you have decided on your brand goal, it is time that you define your brand strategy. Your brand strategy involves everything from how you want people to view your product to how you want to promote it. For example, if you want to build a brand that targets the upper-income segment, then you will have to price your product or service accordingly while also conveying why your product or service is special.

Connecting with Webmasters

An integral part of building a brand through social media marketing is connecting with your peers. Doing this is not all that difficult as long as you know who to reach out to. This leaves us with the question of how to know who to reach out to. Doing this through social media is a bit difficult, as you can either connect with influencers or reach out to the customer service teams that are responsible for maintaining the social media presence of your peer. The best way to do this is by finding out the main websites of the brands similar to yours that also have a social media presence; find out details about their website and then approach the brains of the operation, which would be the website owner of the particular brand.

Two of the best tools for this job is WHOis.net and WHOIS Lookup. When you search by the website address, these websites provide you with data regarding who owns a particular domain name, the SEO score, IP history, response code, when it was purchased, and when it is due to expire. By combining these data sets alone, you can figure out whether reaching out to that particular brand owner is viable or not. Other than this, you can also reach out to them through other means, which will be covered later on in the book.

Reaching out to website owners is crucial because of two things: SEO link building (which we will discuss later) and coming into an agreement to interchange social media posts and advertisements on each other's social media pages. Once you have built a successful network, you may find that your social media organic reach has skyrocketed.

Conclusion

If you want to end 2019 on a high note and be successful on social media in 2020, you are going to need to get to the front of these marketing trends as quickly as you can, and grow with them throughout the rest of the year.

Starting your 2020 marketing strategies right now, halfway through 2019, is going to give you the opportunity to learn how to apply these strategies effectively so that in 2020 you are already more experienced than the majority of businesses out there. This is a crucial step in growing your success, so do not overlook the value of staying ahead of the trend and growing your platform for 2020, right now in 2019.

In this book, we aspired to give you the best marketing advice to help you leverage social media even more and grow your brand massively in the coming months. Whether you are a retail brand, a service-based brand, or a growing influencer, getting on social media and using it properly is going to be the ultimate opportunity for you to get in front of your audience and make waves. Now, you have all of the tools that you need to understand how the four primary social media platforms can be leveraged in 2020 so that you can rise to the top faster than ever before.

As you begin to create and apply your 2020 business strategy, make sure that you really focus on making it personal and unique to you or your brand. Remember, authentic and genuine expression truly is the future of social media marketing, so no matter how professional your brand might be, there will need to be a personal edge in there if you are going to succeed with marketing online. You can ensure that your strategy is authentic by reviewing it after it has been made to ensure that it accurately reflects your brand, your image, and your goals. If it does not, make the necessary adaptations to create that personalized experience, and then begin to apply your strategies to your marketing efforts.

Thank you again for purshing this book! I hope you have gotten adequate information and this book was able to help you start a refutable business online that guarantee passive income.

Finally, if you enjoyed this book, then I'd like to ask you for a favor, would you be kind enough to leave a review for this book on Amazon? It'd be greatly appreciated!

Check my other Kindle book here: Passive Income: Step-By-Step Guide To Make You Expert In Making Money Online. Don't Work For Money, Let The Money Work For You.

Imagine, rather than you working for money you instead made every dollar work for you 40hrs a week. Better still, imagine each and every dollar working for you 24/7 i.e. 168hrs/week. Figuring out the best ways you can make money work for you is an important step on the road to wealth creation.

Passive income is income generated from a trade or business, which does not require the earner to participate. It is often investment income (i.e. income that is not obtained through working) but not exclusively. The central tenet of this type of income is that it can expect to continue whether you continue working or not. As you near retirement you are most definitely seeking to replace earned income with passive, unearned income. The secret to wealth creation earlier on in life is passive income; positive cash-flow generated by assets that you control or own.

One of the reasons people find it difficult to make the leap from earned income to more passive sources of income is that the entire education system is actually pretty much designed to teach us to do a job and hence rely largely on earned income. This works for governments as this kind of income generates large volumes of tax but will not work for you if you're focus is on how to become rich and wealth building. However, to become rich and create wealth you will be re☐uired to cross the chasm from relying on earned income only. So find yourself some time and build your empire, and to do just that, you need this book.

https://www.amazon.com/dp/B07WN16Y3C/

Check my other Kindle book here: JOB INTERVIEW: HOW TO SECURE AND GUARANTEE THE JOB. GUIDE TO PREPARE YOU TO LAND YOUR DREAM JOB. MORE THAN 50 QUESTIONS TO ASSIST YOU FOR THE INTERVIEW

The key to success is to treat the interview as a project, for which you must gather information, make decisions on feasibility, set objectives, identify the resources needed, draw up a plan of action, and manage the project carefully through to closure. In simple terms, you must be professionally prepared for the interview, in order to have the optimum chance of success.

Showing up for a job interview can be pretty intimidating, especially when it's for a company that really interests you. There is nothing like sitting in the hot seat for an hour as your potential boss asks you every question under the sun.

The job interview is where you win or lose the offer. Even the world's best resume and cover letter won't save you if you commit common, critical mistakes. The REAL way to win an interview is by taking just a few extra steps before it even starts so you can craft the perfect answers, display high levels of competence, and get the job every time.

https://www.amazon.com/gp/product/B07WS2DLP3/

Thank you and good luck!

www.ingramcontent.com/pod-product-compliance
Lightning Source LLC
Chambersburg PA
CBHW030540220526
45463CB00007B/2920